101 Ways to Soothe a Crying Baby

J. PEINKOFER, A.C.S.W./L.C.S.W.

CB
CONTEMPORARY BOOKS

Library of Congress Cataloging-in-Publication Data

Peinkofer, Jim.
 101 ways to soothe a crying baby / Jim Peinkofer.
 p. cm.
 ISBN 0-8092-9842-2
 1. Infants—Care. 2. Crying in infants. I. Title.
HQ774.P44 2000
649'.122—dc21 99-88337
 CIP

Cover design by Monica Baziuk
Interior design by Susan H. Hartman
Cover and interior illustrations copyright ©Joan Parazette

Published by Contemporary Books
A division of NTC/Contemporary Publishing Group, Inc.
4255 West Touhy Avenue, Lincolnwood (Chicago), Illinois 60712-1975 U.S.A.
Copyright © 2000 by Jim Peinkofer
Printed in the United States of America
International Standard Book Number: 0-8092-9842-2

00 01 02 03 04 05 LB 14 13 12 11 10 9 8 7 6 5 4 3 2 1

INTRODUCTION

Caring for a baby is a labor of love. The experience is very challenging as well. Caring for a baby that is crying can be emotionally frustrating for a parent or other caregiver.

This book is written for individuals who care for babies; it offers options to use when a baby's crying persists. These techniques can be used separately or in combination with each other. They work well and make caregiving more enriching.

One of the more dramatic and unfortunate aspects of society is physical child abuse. Perpetrators (both men and women) will typically claim that abuse occurred because there were no options for them when the baby cried. Here are 101 options—all positive.

ACKNOWLEDGMENTS

Certain persons have guided me along life's road and their influence has been key in the formation of concepts presented in this book. I would like to thank the following people:

My parents, Richard and Alda, for their positivity and encouragement

My brother, Bob, and his wife, Karen, for being my initial role models for good parenting

Greg Bishop of Bishop and Associates for coming up with the idea of Boot Camp

for New Dads and broadening the
program to the rest of the country
where I was able to be a part of it

Rob Taylor and Kara Leverte of NTC/
Contemporary Publishing Group for
allowing this book to come to life

Finally, I'd like to express my deep
gratitude and love to my wife and soul mate,
Tina, who helped me be the parent and
person I am today; and to my son, Jacob,
who allowed his dad to struggle as well as
succeed during his times of crying. You both
teach me every day. This one's for you.

THE FIRST WORD

Remember—it is never OK to shake
or strike your baby!

DISCOMFORT

*Babies cry mainly because they are
uncomfortable. Such discomfort can be
for any number of basic reasons—hunger,
temperature, stomach gas, etc.
Babies cry to communicate to an adult
that they need something—now.*

1 Pick Up Your Baby

The act of picking up and holding is sometimes the last thing parents and others consider when their baby is crying. Make it the first thing you do. Many people worry about spoiling a baby by picking him or her up too much. Yet, babies under the age of six months do not have the mind-set to cry deliberately to get someone to pick them up. Studies have shown that in countries where babies are frequently held and carried they cry *less*.

2 **Breast-Feed Your Baby**
Hunger is the main reason a baby will cry. Comforting arms and a warm breast soothe wonderfully. Breast-feeding offers so many health benefits to both Mom and baby. If you are experiencing any trouble feeding by breast, there may be a lactation consultant in your community to help. Dad's encouragement has been found to make a difference in the success of breast-feeding.

3 Watch What Foods You Eat if Breast-Feeding

Your baby may react unfavorably when you eat certain foods. Avoid spicy food or foods known to be a family allergy. Avoid stimulants, such as caffeine. Alcohol should never be consumed.

4 Offer a Bottle of Formula

Babies who are bottle-fed will cry for the same reason breast-fed babies cry—they are hungry! Moms and dads can take turns preparing a bottle and feeding. There are a few things to watch for: always make sure the exact mixture is followed, check for a lukewarm temperature, and never use a microwave to heat a bottle. Feeding time is a wonderful time to bond.

5 Change the Type of Formula

Some babies have a preference for certain kinds of formula. Some babies also may be allergic or unable to tolerate certain kinds of formula. The right formula should make for a pleasant feeding experience, not an irritable one.

6 Change a Bottle's Nipple Size or Type

A nipple that doesn't keep up with a hungry baby's demands can cause a lot of frustration. Getting too much milk at once can cause a baby distress as well. Check the appropriateness of a nipple's hole, and make sure the nipple does not regularly collapse.

7 Feed Your Baby on Demand

Young infants should be fed anytime they are hungry. As your baby grows, a feeding schedule can be set. For now, anticipate feeding your baby every few hours.

8 Prepare Your Environment Before Feeding

A baby interrupted during a feeding is an unhappy baby. Make sure you have enough pillows around you to prop your arms while feeding, some water or juice to drink, and the TV remote.

9 Burp Your Baby

Babies do not have a natural ability to get rid of air built up in the stomach from eating, so they need some help. Excess air can make your baby cry. Burping your baby regularly throughout the process of feeding helps avoid discomfort. The process of burping works by applying firm taps or upward strokes on your baby's back after each breast or after two to four ounces of formula.

10 Gently "Bicycle" Your Baby's Legs

This motion helps your baby relieve gas pain.

11 Change Your Baby's Position to Relieve Gas

Simply moving your baby into a different position can help him or her relieve excess gas.

12 Swaddle Your Baby

After being in the womb for nine months, the wide-open world can be scary for your baby. Being swaddled helps your baby feel secure in the first month after being born. Swaddling, or wrapping your baby in a light blanket, is an art that can be easily learned and can successfully soothe your baby.

13 Change Your Baby's Diaper

A wet or dirty diaper is obviously uncomfortable. Your baby may cry to let you know that it is time for a new one. Babies require at least six diaper changes per day. This is why Mom and Dad soon become experts at the art of diaper changing!

14 Buy a Diaper-Wipes Warmer

A cold diaper wipe is probably very disconcerting to a baby. A wipes warmer is inexpensive and worth the effort to help your baby feel content with the process of diaper changing.

15 Check for Diaper Rash

Diaper rash can be particularly distressing for your baby. Lukewarm baths can help soothe tender skin rash. Air dry and then coat the rash with diaper ointment. Use ointment only if a rash is seen. Stay away from using powder, which can get into your baby's lungs.

16 Check for Foreign Objects in Your Baby's Clothes or Diaper

The smallest objects in a baby's diaper or clothing can be painful and very uncomfortable. Though rare, this does happen.

17 Change Your Baby's Clothes

After a day of wearing the same clothes, a baby might be uncomfortable. Also, new clothing may even be slightly abrasive to tender skin. Remember to always wash items before your baby wears them.

18 Check if Your Baby's Clothing Is Too Tight

Something loose-fitting and soft may be just what your baby needs to settle down.

19 Check if Your Baby Is Too Cold

Temperature is a very important issue in keeping your baby comfortable and soothed. A baby's skin is very tender. If your baby's skin feels cool to the touch, try warmer clothes.

20 **Check if Your Baby Is Too Hot**
A baby should never be overly hot—in fact, this can be dangerous. If your baby is warm to the touch, check the amount of clothing he or she is wearing. Taking your baby's temperature can rule out fever.

21 **Check for Hair Twists on Toes**
Hair or fabric from baby socks that is wrapped around your baby's toes can be dangerous and painful.

22 Avoid Bright Lights at Night

If you are teaching your baby nighttime from daytime, bright lights can be harsh. Low lighting helps supplement the natural darkness of night.

23 Limit Overstimulating Situations

Most babies do not like over-stimulating people or situations. Being passed back and forth between a variety of people may cause your baby to cry. Limit inundating your baby with new people and things—he or she will have plenty of time to learn.

24 Avoid Soap in Eyes at Bath Time

Take care while rinsing soap and shampoo from your baby's head and face. The chemicals in some brands can irritate your baby's eyes.

25 Keep Pets Away

Pets can scare babies and can be intrusive as well. Take care to always monitor pets around your baby and keep them at a safe distance.

26 Don't Allow Smoke in Your Home

Smoke is a health hazard, especially for an infant. The risk of SIDS (sudden infant death syndrome) or respiratory problems is higher in homes where there is smoke. Breathing noxious fumes from smoke can be very irritating to your baby.

27 Take Your Baby's Temperature

Your baby may be crying because he or she is ill. There are many ways to take a baby's temperature: rectally, regular axillary (under arm), digital axillary, digital pacifier, and digital in the ear. Digital thermometers are made to show accurate temperature. When using a rectal thermometer, subtract 1 degree. For a regular axillary thermometer, add 1 degree.

28 Check for Teething Pain

As babies grow, teeth will break through their gums—a typically painful experience. You can feel swelling by lightly running a clean finger along the gum line. Try using an analgesic gel to help alleviate this pain.

29 Plan for Reactions to Shots

Anticipate your baby being extra fussy after getting a vaccination. Some parents are even hesitant to have their babies get vaccinated, because of the pain of the needle and potential reactions that may follow. Benefits of having your baby vaccinated clearly outweigh the temporary pain and follow-up risks. Your pediatrician should give you written information on reactions from getting a vaccine. Take this home and prepare to provide extra comfort measures.

30 Call Your Pediatrician if You Suspect Illness

Your baby may need to be seen by your pediatrician if he or she continues to cry inconsolably. Doctors can guide you through rough times by over-the-phone assessments. If you still are not satisfied after such an assessment, have your baby checked at a local hospital emergency room.

COMFORT AND JOY

*A baby's needs are simple. Most needs
focus around basic comfort. Babies enjoy
happy things and people in their
environment. Select certain times for
stimulation and other times for quiet and
comforting, close, physical contact.*

31 Give Your Baby a Lukewarm Bath

After your baby's umbilical cord has fallen off, he or she is ready for a bath. Make sure the water temperature is lukewarm and comfortable enough to soothe your baby. Be careful when using soap—a baby's skin can become very slippery and his or her eyes can be sensitive to chemicals. Always stay right with your baby during a bath.

32 Massage Your Baby

A gentle massage on your baby's back, arms, and legs can be comforting. There are many books and workshops on infant massage. Learn what you can, and use these techniques on your baby.

33 Lay Your Baby on Your Chest

Skin-to-skin contact can be very soothing for your baby. Your slow breathing and the sound of your heartbeat can lull even the fussiest of babies. This contact is great for you too.

34 Offer a Pacifier

Pacifiers can work wonders when baby really needs to be soothed. Use this device sparingly, especially when Mom is trying to establish breast-feeding. Using a pacifier when a baby is not crying may defeat the purpose of its use.

35 **Carry Your Baby in a Sling**
Young infants can ride comfortably
in a baby sling. The enclosed space can make
your baby feel very secure. A sling also frees
up Mom and Dad's hands, which can be very
helpful around the house.

36 **Hold Your Baby**
Humans, especially babies, have an
instinctual need to be held. This is tender,
loving care at its best.

37 Offer Your Baby His or Her Fingers to Suck

Instead of immediately reaching for a pacifier, try a natural one. Babies are not aware of their own bodies for many months. Remind your baby that his or her own fingers can give comfort. Gently guide several fingers to your baby's mouth during a time of crying and see if there might be some interest in them.

38 Give Attention to Your Baby

Never ignore your baby when he or she cries, especially in the first several months. A baby completely depends on you, and you should be at his or her beck and call.

39 Offer a Clipped, Clean Pinky to Suck

During extra fussy times, an adult finger can be a great natural pacifier. Make sure you don't have long or sharp fingernails—they may cut the roof of a baby's mouth. Always clean your hands thoroughly with lots of soap and hot water before you put any fingers in your baby's mouth.

40 **Make Happy Eye Contact**
Connecting eye-to-eye during a time of crying can distract your baby. Don't get too close or too far away, as young babies have a visual range of around one to two feet. Stay happy—your baby will be happy too!

41 Support Your Baby's Back and Head

Newborns and young infants have large heads and weak neck muscles. Keeping your baby supported can help prevent sudden movements that may be startling to your baby. This kind of support also lets your baby feel secure.

42 Put Your Baby in a Front Carrier

Carrying your baby in a front carrier is another way to make your baby feel secure. The motion of being transported from place to place is comforting, too.

43 Kiss Your Baby
Gentle kisses on your baby's face and head can keep tense crying episodes lighthearted.

44 Cuddle and Nestle Your Baby
Face-to-face contact will feel good to both you and your baby.

45 Stroke Your Baby's Forehead

Light fingertip strokes along your baby's forehead during crying is a pleasant, soothing sensation.

46 Kiss the Bottom of Your Baby's Feet

The soles of your baby's feet are extra sensitive. Light kisses on them can turn a challenging situation into a happy one.

47 **Show Your Baby a Silly Face**
Babies respond to exaggerated facial movements. The sillier the better!

48 **Blow Gently on Your Baby's Forehead**
Wide-open-mouth crying generally can be lessened through gentle blowing on your baby's forehead. The sensation of breath can cause your baby to stop and take a breath.

49 Bring Your Baby to Bed for a Short Time

Snuggle with your baby in bed to help soothe an episode of crying. Such close contact makes for a wonderful bonding time. Never place your baby on a waterbed. Also, take care that you give your baby enough space to lie comfortably. To prevent anything from going wrong, place your baby back in his or her bassinet or crib before you go to sleep.

Music to the Ears

A baby's hearing is functioning by the third month in utero. Because of this, your baby is used to certain sounds—some more comforting than others. Discover with your baby which noises and sounds he or she likes best, and use these to your benefit when you need them most.

50 Reassure with Soft Words

Words like, "it's ok," and "there, there" are well-known examples of comforting phrases. These words work well on Mom and Dad, too.

51 Sing Softly

For generations, human voices have been able to soothe crying babies through singing. Lullabies have been written solely for this purpose.

52 **Play Quiet Music**
Babies love classical music that has soothing melodies. If you or your partner can't carry a tune, try an easy-listening CD or tape.

53 **Whistle a Quiet Tune**
Whistling is a good supplement to singing. This especially rings true during a 3:00 A.M. crying session when you don't feel like singing. Just make sure the whistle is soft, melodic, and slow.

54 **Hum**

Another category of music produced by the human voice is humming. The pleasant vibrations caused by humming make it one of the more soothing strategies a parent or another caregiver can use with a baby.

55 Hum in Low Tones Against Your Baby's Head

Dads have an advantage with this soothing feature. Hum in low, soft tones that resonate through your baby's skull. This humming is very lulling to a baby and makes a great bonding activity.

56 Play a Heartbeat Tape

For nine months, a baby has heard his or her mother's heartbeat. Audiotapes are available that replicate a human heartbeat set to a musical background. The sound of something familiar can reassure your baby.

57 Offer a Musical Stuffed Animal

Something soft, pleasant to look at, and musical makes for an enjoyable combination.

58 Play a Windup Music Box

Music boxes are handy to own because they are freestanding and time-limited. If you need a break from your baby's crying, you can wind a music box. This allows you to take several minutes for yourself. You can then check on your baby and wind up the box again if needed.

59 Run a Vacuum Cleaner

This is the first device in a series of examples of white noise—any sound that produces a loud, neutral, masking noise. Running a vacuum can stop a crying baby almost immediately. It seems to hypnotize a baby. A vacuum is not a bothersome sound to a baby—rather, a vacuum can put a baby to sleep!

60 **Run a Shower**
The sound of running water creates a distracting and curious rhythm to a crying baby. Sit on the floor of your bathroom with your baby and run a cold or lukewarm shower—for noise only.

61 **Run a Sink Faucet**
This is an alternative to the above method, with the same soothing benefits.

62 Play Static on TV or the Radio

Static is the ultimate white-noise producer. The sound should not be excessively loud, but just enough to get your baby's attention.

63 Run a Dishwasher

Dishwashers have various cycles and various white-noise rhythms. Plan efficiently to run your dishwasher when you need it!

64 Avoid Loud Noises

Harsh, sudden noises can be very disturbing and easily cause your baby to start crying. Look for ways to avoid these, and tell others in the home to do the same.

MOTION

Motion is one of the best ways to calm your crying baby. It doesn't matter if your baby is moving or the outside world is moving—motion is always an intriguing experience.

65 Do Slight Knee Bends While Holding Your Baby

"Elevator" movement is another successful motion to use with your crying baby. Moms who have recently given birth should wait several weeks before trying this movement.

66 Gently Rock Your Baby Side to Side

Sway to-and-fro to create a special kind of motion that is very soothing to a baby.

67 Take a Drive with Your Baby

Any time of day or night, driving has a classic sleep-inducing effect on babies. Make sure your baby is secure in a car seat (rear-facing in the middle of the backseat), and enjoy an easy car ride.

68 Rock Your Baby in a Rocker

A rocking chair, particularly a glider rocker, is a great investment. Middle of the night rocking sessions are relaxing for Mom or Dad and soothing to a baby.

69 Use an Electric or Windup Swing

The motion of a rhythmic swing lulls crying babies. Make sure you strap your baby in and do not leave him or her unattended. Limit the amount of time your baby is in a swing. Again, babies need to be held, not just left swinging.

70 **Take Your Baby for a Stroller Ride**

Next to the motion of a car ride, a ride in a stroller is the next best thing for calming your baby.

71 **Dance Gently**

Dancing is fun for Mom or Dad and can allow for a variety of soothing movements for your baby.

72 Swing Your Baby in a Car Seat

Grasp the upright, locked-in-place, handle of a car seat and give your baby a special ride. Movements can be done at your own pace.

73 Walk with Your Baby in a Large Circle

Hold or carry your crying baby in a darkened room and walk slowly around in a large circle—ten to twenty times, or more!

74 Place Your Baby in a Car Seat on Top of a Dryer Running on No or Low Heat and Watch Carefully

The hum and vibration of a running dryer is another classic sleep-inducer. Take special care with this technique and never leave your baby unattended.

RHYTHM OF THE NIGHT

Babies respond to rhythmic sounds,
patterns, and movements. Repetition
becomes soothing as well as distracting
for them. Parents can create easy rhythms
any time of day or night.

75 **Pat Your Baby's Back**
Gentle taps on your baby's back while carrying or rocking him or her can be reassuring. This is a different action than burping.

76 **Speak in a Rhythmic Pattern**
Rhymes, poetry, and simple rhythmic talking can soothe your baby. It also helps teach the motion of language.

77 Coo or Babble Back

In the midst of a crying spell, talk with your baby in a language he or she understands—baby talk.

78 Watch a Sporting Event on TV with Your Baby

Babies like watching and listening to any sporting event on TV. Watching a player or ball is a good way for your baby to understand patterns and rhythmic movements. It's also a nice distraction for Mom or Dad.

79 Get a Lighted Mobile
All the mechanisms on a lighted
mobile (sounds, lights, and movement) can
help amuse and entertain your baby.

80 Let Your Baby Hear the Ticking
of a Clock or Metronome
The sound of ticking has a tempo both
curious and repetitive for a baby. Make sure
the pace of the clock or metronome is slow
and steady.

81 Read Softly

A calm voice reading a book, newspaper, or magazine can pleasantly engross your baby. Reading is also good for the development of speech and language in your growing baby.

CREATING AN ENVIRONMENT

Look at your home living environment. Is it chaotic or mellow? Is it in disarray or can you find things in a hurry? Ask yourself what kind of environment you want to live in with your baby. Does this type of arrangement have an effect on the frequency of your baby's crying?

82 Use a Timer Night-Light

Night-lights can help your baby feel comforted while falling asleep. Recent research has suggested that using night-lights throughout the night can predispose infants and children to nearsighted vision later in life. A night-light on a timer or switch is suggested as an alternative.

83 Turn the Lights Off

Babies can be soothed simply by providing some "mood lighting." Dim lights create a soft environment that can help your baby be at peace.

84 Show Your Baby Different Objects

Holding up toys or other unusual objects to your crying baby may be a good distraction. Make sure the objects you use are soft, clean, and in good shape, and make pleasant sounds. Infants are always curious about different objects—so be creative.

85 Put Your Baby up to a Mirror

Seeing another baby is a wonderful way to stop yours from crying. Babies are very curious about their own reflection in a mirror, and you can have fun pointing out different facial features.

86 Hold Your Baby up to a Window to Watch the World

Objects moving outside help a baby learn about his or her environment. Mom or Dad pointing out a squirrel, a child on a bike, or a big truck going by can help a baby settle down to some pleasant world watching.

87 Play on the Floor with Your Baby

Getting down on the floor with your baby can be great fun. It is also a good way to soothe your baby during a crying spell. Be sure all play activity is done gently, and judge if your baby responds positively to it.

HELP YOURSELF TO
HELP YOUR BABY

*Believe it or not, you can do certain
things for yourself that will directly help
soothe your baby. Parenting can be
fulfilling and frustrating at the same time.
Make sure you are doing OK before you
help your baby.*

88 Take Soothing Turns with Your Partner

This is termed "tag-team parenting." When you need a break from your crying baby—hand him or her to your partner. Do something positive for yourself, and then take another turn in a half hour.

89 Relax Yourself

Research has shown that the anxiety level of the adult caregiver is amplified in a baby. Babies can pick up on emotions. If you are overly stressed because your baby is crying, it will not help your baby settle down. Breathe deeply, smile, and visualize a peaceful place in your mind. Relax.

90 After Several Months, Set a Schedule for Your Baby

Newborns' needs are often immediate ones. When your baby begins to extend sleep time through the night and seems to be ready for a schedule, go ahead and set one. Your baby will then know when it is time for food, bed, etc. He or she might not get overly fussy if comfort is right around the corner. Remember to be flexible—there are no hard and fast rules with infants.

91 Look for a Crying Pattern and Prepare for It

Babies have certain cries for certain needs. Parents can usually pick up on which cry is for which need.

92 Treat Yourself

When you have had little sleep, provided constant caregiving, and met other stressful demands, take a break. Treat yourself to something special. It might be a simple walk outside or dinner at your favorite restaurant. Every now and then, give yourself a special moment to look forward to, either alone or with someone else.

93 Keep Your Mood Upbeat

When you are with a crying baby, laughter *is* the best medicine. Frustration, or even anger, can be a tempting emotion. Instead, keep your heart light and as happy as you are able. You supply all the needs of your baby, and that job can be very rewarding if you let it.

94 **Support Your Partner**
If you have a partner helping you raise your baby, he or she may do things differently than you. Another person's soothing techniques may not be the same as yours. If your partner is providing the safest care he or she knows—support such efforts. Your positive words can make a difference in the care provided to your baby.

95 Avoid Conflict at Home

The last thing you want along with the demands of caregiving is conflict. You and your partner may be short-fused because of lack of sleep or other stresses. Do not take it out on each other. A negative home environment will create more crying and tension in your baby. Instead, nurture your relationship and celebrate yourself as a family.

96 Identify Cues Before Your Baby Cries

Prepare yourself for signs of crying. Some babies progress steadily toward outright crying. They fuss, then whimper, then cry, and then scream. Anticipate these signs and satisfy your baby before crying becomes hard to control.

97 Think "Short-Term"

Understand that most issues that frustrate you as parents will usually be short-term, and soon you will be back on the right track. This, too, shall pass.

98 Create a Peaceful, Warm Home Environment

Part of what can keep a baby relatively placid is the type of environment that surrounds him or her. Pleasant lighting, smells, music, and voices all lend themselves to pleasant living.

WHAT OTHERS CAN DO

When other people in your support network of family and friends offer to help you care for your baby, take them up on it! Caregiving allows others a chance to know your baby and to experience some of the joy that has come to you in a little package.

99 Let Others Give You a Break

Even the best parents need a break from caregiving duties. Other people can provide this for you. Make sure you are completely comfortable with the person who is providing the respite. Then go ahead and relax for a few hours!

100 Inform Others About Ways to Soothe Your Baby

This is a vital issue for others who may be caring for your baby. Buy an extra copy of this book for them so they may be ready to soothe if there is an episode of crying. Explain to them what your baby likes and dislikes. Tell them never to discipline or shake your baby. And, if they have any needs or questions, they should call you.

101 Don't Toss or Play Roughly with Your Baby

Relatives and friends who want to play with your baby in such a manner should be kindly informed not to do so. Babies are fragile. They need support and loving arms. Rough play can alarm a baby and asks for trouble, as it is potentially hazardous. Accidents can happen.

THE LAST WORD

Finally, if all else fails, let your baby cry him- or herself to sleep—he or she is safe.

ABOUT THE AUTHOR

Jim Peinkofer is a licensed clinical social worker on a pediatric unit in a midwestern hospital. He is also a childbirth educator and team teaches with his wife, Christine. He has degrees from Hartwick College, Rochester Institute of Technology, and University of Buffalo. In 1997, he founded Peinkofer Associates, a health-care consultation agency specializing in Shaken Infant Syndrome prevention and education and positive parenting. In addition to his wife, he lives with two stepsons, Matthew and Tom, and son Jacob.